SPORTS SCIENCE

Rockets

Science at Work in
SNOWBOARDING

By Richard Hantula

**Science and Curriculum
Consultant:**
Debra Voege, M.A.,
Science Curriculum
Resource Teacher

mc **Marshall Cavendish**
Benchmark
New York

Other Marshall Cavendish Offices:
Marshall Cavendish International (Asia) Private Limited, 1 New Industrial Road, Singapore 536196 • Marshall Cavendish International (Thailand) Co Ltd. 253 Asoke, 12th Flr, Sukhumvit 21 Road, Klongtoey Nua, Wattana, Bangkok 10110, Thailand • Marshall Cavendish (Malaysia) Sdn Bhd, Times Subang, Lot 46, Subang Hi-Tech Industrial Park, Batu Tiga, 40000 Shah Alam, Selangor Darul Ehsan, Malaysia

Marshall Cavendish is a trademark of Times Publishing Limited

All websites were available and accurate when this book was sent to press.

Library of Congress Cataloging-in-Publication Data
Hantula, Richard.
      Science at work in snowboarding / Richard Hantula.
         p. cm. — (Sports science)
      Includes index.
      Summary: "Explains how the laws of science, especially physics, are at work in the sport of snowboarding"—Provided by publisher.
      ISBN 978-1-60870-590-0 (print) — ISBN 978-1-60870-734-8 (ebook)
    1. Snowboarding—Juvenile literature. 2. Physics—Juvenile literature. I. Title.
GV857.S57H36 2012
796.939—dc22   2010052777

Developed for Marshall Cavendish Benchmark by RJF Publishing LLC (www.RJFpublishing.com)
Design: Westgraphix LLC/Tammy West
Photo Research: Edward A. Thomas

Cover: Shaun White soars above the half-pipe at the 2010 Winter Olympics.

The photographs in this book are used by permission and through the courtesy of:
Front Cover: Mark J. Terrill/AP Images.
Alamy: © Action Plus Sports Images, 29. AP Images: Darryl Dyck, CP, 15; Marcio Sanchez, 24. Getty Images: Robert Beck/Sports Illustrated, 4; Doug Pensinger, 6; Cameron Spencer, 11; Jamie Squire, 18; MARTIN BUREAU/AFP, 23. Landov: Kyodo, 5, 22. Newscom: ADRIAN DENNIS/AFP/Getty Images, 12; William Stevenson, 17; Marc Piscotty/Icon SMI 141, 26.

Printed in Malaysia (T)
135642

CONTENTS

Chapter One
Playing Tricks
with Gravity 4

Chapter Two
Faster, Faster, Turn, Turn . . 12

Chapter Three
Riding on Water,
Stopping on a Dime 18

Chapter Four
An Extreme Sport 24

Glossary 30
Find Out More 31
Index 32

Words defined in the glossary are in
bold type the first time they appear
in the text.

CHAPTER ONE
Playing Tricks with Gravity

Mercedes Nicoll of Canada competes in the half-pipe at the 2010 Winter Olympics.

Picture a big tube or pipe that's missing its top half. That's what a snowboarder's **half-pipe** is like. A boarder starts at the top of one side. He or she "rides" the board to the bottom of the half-pipe and then keeps on going up the other side. With enough speed, the boarder flies higher than the top edge, then starts coming back down into the pipe. While still in the air, the boarder does a **trick**—twisting or turning or even flipping head over heels.

At the 2010 Winter Olympic Games in Canada, the half-pipe was huge. It was 550 feet (168 meters) long. The walls were 22 feet (6.8 meters) high. American snowboarder Shaun White rode his board to as high as

SHAUN WHITE

Shaun White is famous for his amazing tricks high in the air over the half-pipe. He is also famous for his red hair, which he wears down to his shoulders. The hair earned him the nickname "The Flying Tomato." He himself says he prefers the nickname "Animal." That's the name of the wild drummer in a Muppet band.

White was born in San Diego, California, in 1986. As a baby, he had a heart problem, and doctors did two operations to fix it. He started snowboarding around the age of six. He was very good at it, and a snowboard company soon signed on as his sponsor. White's snowboarding skills eventually gained him the gold medal in the men's half-pipe in two Winter Olympics—in 2006 and 2010. In the photo at right, he celebrates after a good run in the half-pipe at the 2010 Games.

25 feet (7.6 meters) above the top. He did some amazing tricks and won the gold medal. His most spectacular trick was called the Double McTwist 1260. White did two head-over-heels flips and twisted his body around three and a half times.

Moved by the Force

Tricks in half-pipes are not the only things snowboarders do. Some boarders do tricks during jumps. Some like to slide over rails and other objects not covered with snow. Some love to race down snowy slopes. When they come to an obstacle, they steer around it. If the obstacle is flat enough, they may even ride over it.

Snowboarding is not always done on snow. Shown here: Jamie Anderson slides a rail during a Winter X Games competition.

Fun Names

Snowboarding is a mixture of skateboarding and surfing. It uses a lot of words from those two sports. Some of them may seem weird to people who don't know the sports.

Just as in surfing, standing on the board with the left foot in front is called regular. Standing with the right foot in front is called goofy. Like skateboarders, snowboarders do jumps called ollies and nollies. In an ollie, you jump up with the board by first pushing down on its back end. The move is named after its inventor, skateboarder Alan "Ollie" Gelfand. In a nollie you jump up by first pushing down on the board's nose, or front end. The name comes from adding the letter *n* (for "nose") to *ollie*.

The "McTwist" in Shaun White's Double McTwist 1260 is a twisting, flipping move named for its inventor, American skateboarder Mike McGill. In the McTwist the boarder spins around one and a half times, or 540 degrees. (One spin all the way around would be 360 degrees. Half a spin is 180 degrees.) White did two McTwists and added an extra half spin. As a result, he spun around three and a half times, or 1,260 degrees. Actually, White said he wanted to change the name of the trick to "The Tomahawk," after a huge steak he enjoyed.

No matter what they do, snowboarders make use of a very important **force**: Earth's **gravity**. A force is anything that causes a push or a pull. Earth's gravity pulls things downward—that is, toward the center of Earth. It is gravity that pulls a snowboarder down a slope.

Gravity is always at work. If a snowboarder happens to be gliding up a half-pipe wall, gravity keeps pulling. It makes the boarder go slower and slower. At some point the boarder stops rising and starts to come down.

Science Helps

A branch of science called **physics** can explain how snowboarders do what they do. Physics studies the motion of objects—including snowboarders. It also deals with all the forces, such as gravity, that act on objects. Knowing a little physics can help snowboarders understand what they need to do in order to get better at riding their boards.

In the 1600s the English scientist Isaac Newton described three rules, or laws, that explain the motion of all ordinary objects.

The first of Newton's laws of motion says that a moving object will keep on going in the same direction and at the same speed unless some force causes a change in its motion. The law also applies to an object that is not moving at all. Such an object is said to be at rest. Its speed is zero. The only way the speed will become greater than zero is if some force acts on the object.

Think of a snowboarder shooting up out of a half-pipe. The first law of motion says that the boarder will keep on going upward forever—unless some force acts. Of course, gravity does its job. It is always acting. Because of gravity, the boarder actually goes only a little way above the half-pipe before starting to come down.

Or think of a snowboarder standing still at the flat top of a snowy slope. Gravity keeps pulling, but the ground stops the boarder from dropping down into Earth. The ground offers enough **resistance** to balance out gravity's pull. As a result, the snowboarder is at rest. But if a new force acts, it may change the situation.

Suppose the boarder pushes hard against the ground with one foot. This force starts the boarder going downhill. Now

PHYSICS FACT

First Law of Motion

If an object is at rest, it will stay at rest unless a force acts on it. If an object is moving, it will keep on moving in the same direction and at the same speed unless a force acts on it.

the boarder is in motion. Actually, the ground continues to stop the boarder from dropping down into Earth. But because the hill slopes downward, some of gravity's downward pull makes the snowboarder go faster and faster down the slope.

A Simpler Way to Say the First Law

By using the idea of **velocity**, the first law of motion can be said more simply. People sometimes use *velocity* to mean just "speed." Physicists, however, use the word in a special way. For them, the velocity of an object is the combination of the object's speed and its direction. If *velocity* is used in this way, the first law's description of a moving object becomes simpler and easier to remember: an object in motion will keep on moving at the same velocity unless a force acts on it.

Keeping the Center in the Right Spot

Another physics idea that is important in snowboarding is the **center of gravity**. Boarders do a lot of different things to help control their board's movement. They shift their weight from their toes to their heels and back, or from one foot to the other. They move their arms, legs, and head. They twist their body. All these actions may change how gravity affects their body. The force of gravity's pull on the body doesn't change. But the body's shape does. So does the arrangement of weight inside their body.

To see how this idea works, stand on one leg while holding the foot of the other leg just an inch or so (about 2 centimeters) off the floor. You probably can stand up fine. Next, stretch out the raised leg in front of you, and stretch out both arms in the same direction. You probably feel a little off balance, or unstable. (Be careful not to fall!) Your body still has the same **mass,** or amount of matter, as before, but its shape has changed. It now seems to react differently to gravity's pull.

Actually, gravity acts on an object as if all of the object's mass—all the matter in it—were concentrated at one spot inside it. This spot is the center of gravity. The center of gravity often does not lie at the exact center of an object. Its position depends on the object's shape and on how the object's mass is arranged inside that shape. When you stretched out your leg and arms, you changed the position of your center of gravity.

Ordinarily, a person's center of gravity tends to be located somewhere in the hip region. With practice, snowboarders can develop a good sense of where their center of gravity is at any particular moment. They must

See the Seesaw

Changing the position or shape of your body while on a snowboard changes the arrangement of your weight. In other words, it changes the position of your center of gravity.

The same thing happens when you change the arrangement of weight on a seesaw. If no one sits on it, its center of gravity is in the middle. The seesaw is evenly balanced. Suppose a kid gets on one end, and an adult (who is heavier) gets on the other. This shifts the seesaw's center of gravity toward the adult. The end with the adult

moves down, and the end with the kid goes up. Now suppose the two people change places. The center of gravity again moves toward the adult. To shift the seesaw's center of gravity back to the middle, the arrangement of weight needs to be changed. This can be done if the adult sits closer to the middle. When the adult moves toward the middle of the seesaw, this action has the same kind of effect—changing the center of gravity—as when a snowboarder changes the position of his or her body.

always be ready to shift it. To avoid falling while going down a slope, they need to keep their center of gravity over the board. It often happens that only one edge of the board is touching the snow. In that case, it is important to keep the center of gravity over that edge.

Bent knees can also help reduce the chances of falling. This is because objects with a low center of gravity are less likely to fall over. Bending the knees helps bring the snowboarder closer to the ground—and lowers the center of gravity.

To avoid falling, snowboarders speeding down a slope need to keep their center of gravity over the board.

CHAPTER TWO

Faster, Faster, Turn, Turn

Canada's Maëlle Ricker does a jump during the women's snowboard cross final at the Winter Olympics in 2010.

S nowboarders doing tricks have to keep control of their balance—and their boards. They need to be able to shift their weight and change the position of their body to make their tricks work.

Snowboarders riding down a slope need to do these things, too. Gravity keeps trying to make them go faster and faster. They, however, may want to slow down. They definitely at some point will want to stop. **Freeriding** snowboarders love natural slopes out in the countryside. If an obstacle such as a tree or a big rock is in their path, they will want to go around it. Obstacles also show up in downhill races such as the snowboard cross and the parallel giant slalom. In the cross, several (usually four) snowboarders speed down a narrow course that has turns and jumps. In the giant slalom, two boarders do turns through a series of gates as they zigzag downhill.

Velocity Changes

Stopping, slowing down, speeding up, turning—all these involve a change in velocity. They all involve a change in the speed or direction of the snowboarder's motion. Physicists have a special name for a change in velocity. They call it **acceleration**. Some people use that word to refer to an increase in speed. But for physicists it may mean any velocity change—an increase or a decrease in speed or a change in direction.

The second of Newton's three laws of motion describes the relation between a force and the acceleration that the force causes in an object. The law says that the amount of acceleration depends both on the strength of the force itself and on the mass of the object. Suppose a force acts on an

PHYSICS FACT

Second Law of Motion

When a force acts on an object, the greater the force, the greater the acceleration it gives to the object. If the same force is used on objects of different masses, objects with less mass receive more acceleration.

object for one second, and then a different, stronger force acts on the same object for one second. The stronger force will produce a greater acceleration. On the other hand, suppose there are two objects with different masses. If the same force is applied to each of them, the object with a smaller mass will receive more acceleration.

Some forces act for just a short time. This is true of the force a snowboarder uses to push off the top of a slope. Earth's gravity is a special sort of force in a couple of ways. For one thing, it is always pulling. For another, it always produces the same acceleration on every object at Earth's surface. In other words, it pulls more strongly on massive objects than on objects with less mass.

Turning Here and There

The fastest way for a snowboarder to go down a mountain is to head straight for the bottom. This is often not a good idea,

Is Weight the Same as Mass?

Weight and mass are not the same thing, but the two are related. Weight is a measure of how strongly gravity pulls on an object. If one object has more mass than another, gravity will pull more strongly on it. As a result, it will weigh more than that second object.

The weight of an object on Earth is determined by Earth's gravity. Suppose this object is taken to the Moon. The object's mass does not change. But its weight does. The object's weight on the Moon will be much less because the Moon's gravity is weaker than Earth's.

On her way to the Olympic gold medal in 2010, Nicolien Sauerbreij of the Netherlands carves a turn during the parallel giant slalom competition.

however. For one thing, the rider may pick up so much speed that it becomes impossible to control the board. For another, there may be obstacles that have to be avoided.

Snowboarders need to make turns of various kinds. For example, in what is called traversing, the snowboarder follows a gradual zigzag path down the slope. Then there's carving, in which the boarder makes quick turns with only the edge of the board in contact with the snow. The edge cuts through the snow like a knife.

Some turns are harder to learn than others, but all turns generally depend on a key basic idea: by leaning and shifting his or her weight, the snowboarder changes the forces his or her feet apply to the board. The result is a change in the direction in which the board goes. In order to carve a turn to the left, for example, the boarder needs to lean left. This applies a leftward force to the board, and the board shifts to the left. It's the second law of motion at work!

Push and Be Pushed

Snowboarders shouldn't try going down a mountain before they know how to stop. Falling down is one way to stop, of course. But since falls can be painful and cause injuries, it's best to know other ways.

Fast and Super Fast

How fast can a snowboarder go? It depends. Imagine a boarder is going down the slope of a high mountain. Gravity's pull never stops, and there's lots of space to build up speed. If the slope is very gradual, however, only a little of gravity's pull goes to make the boarder gain speed. The boarder will gain speed slowly and may not end up going very fast at all. A steep slope offers less resistance to gravity's pull, and the boarder will go faster.

But once the snowboarder starts picking up speed, another force begins offering a lot of resistance. That force, called **drag**, comes from the air. The air tends to slow down any object that moves through it. As the object's speed increases, the strength of the drag also increases. In fact, the drag grows even faster than the speed. Even a snowboarder who dropped off a high cliff wouldn't be able to go any faster than a certain "terminal" velocity. This is the velocity at which the air resistance becomes strong enough to balance the pull of gravity. A snowboarder who reaches terminal velocity can keep going at the same speed but won't be able to increase his or her speed any further.

A snowboarder can reduce drag by becoming more **aerodynamic**. This involves doing things that let the air flow past more smoothly—such as crouching down and wearing special gear. Still, air resistance cannot be eliminated.

Australian snowboarder Darren Powell claims to hold the world record for snowboard speed. In 1999 he reached a speed of slightly more than 125 miles (201 kilometers) an hour at Les Arcs, a mountain ski resort in France.

At such speeds, the chances of a bad accident are high. Most boarders go much slower. A study by one scientist found that the average speed of snowboarders at ski resorts was about 24 miles (39 kilometers) an hour.

One better way to stop is to sideslip. In sideslipping, the boarder turns the snowboard sharply to the side. As the snowboarder continues to skid down hill, the edge of his or her board digs into the snow. This lets the snowboarder take advantage of the third of Newton's laws of motion.

The third law deals with what happens when one object applies a force to another. It says that the second object will at the same time apply a force to the first. The two forces will be equal in strength but opposite in direction.

When the snowboarder riding down a slope does a sideslip, he or she is pushing the board into the snow. The snow obeys the third law

and pushes back. The result of the snow's push is easy to see. This force makes the snowboarder slow down and stop. The result of the snowboarder's push is not as visible. Some of the force of the boarder's push may spray some snow

around. But much of the snowboarder's force is simply absorbed by the ground. The ground is really part of Earth. So the snowboarder is actually pushing on Earth. Earth's mass is enormous. Any acceleration that the snowboarder gives it will be far too small to notice.

A snowboarder going down a steep slope can pick up a lot of speed. Knowing how to stop safely is very important.

CHAPTER THREE

Riding on Water, Stopping on a Dime

Seth Wescott races toward the finish line of the 2010 Olympics men's snowboard cross final.

The weather at the 2010 Winter Olympics was unusually warm and rainy. At times the snow cover in some places turned to slush. Workers did everything they could to keep the snow in good shape for the snowboard cross and other events. Still, there were worries that the surface might be more slippery, and more dangerous, than usual.

About halfway through the final for the men's snowboard cross, American Nate Holland was fighting with Canada's Mike Robertson for the lead. Suddenly Holland lost his balance and wiped out.

After that, Robertson seemed sure to win. But then another American, Seth Wescott, put on a stunning burst of speed. Wescott had begun the race at the back of the pack. He flew past Robertson on the final jump to win the gold. He beat Robertson by less than the length of a snowboard.

Another Key Force

Snowboarders make use of gravity. Air resistance also affects what boarders can do, especially when they go fast. But there is another force that plays a major role in snowboarding. That force, called **friction**, is the resistance that a surface offers to the movement of an object traveling across it.

Snowboarders want the surface of the snow to have some friction. If there is too little friction, the surface will be too slippery, making the snowboard difficult to control. This can happen when melting snow turns to slush or water. It is possible Holland rode over a particularly slippery patch in the men's Olympic snowboard cross final. Canadian Maëlle Ricker, who won the women's snowboard cross, also fell, but luckily for her she did it during a qualifying run, not during the final.

On the other hand, some slipperiness is necessary for the snowboard to move smoothly down a slope. A surface with too much friction will be sticky. It will let the snowboard move only very slowly, and the boarder may not pick up enough **momentum** to do amazing jumps or tricks.

Momentum is a measure of motion. It depends on both mass and velocity. If two boarders have the same mass and the first is going faster than the second, the first one has more momentum. If a heavier snowboarder and a lighter boarder are moving at the same velocity, the heavier one has more momentum. It is because of momentum that a boarder can shoot up above a half-pipe. The boarder

Using Gravity and Momentum

Gravity

Entry Ramp

Snowboarder's Path

A boarder going down a half-pipe wall picks up speed—and momentum—as a result of gravity's pull. As this momentum carries the boarder up the opposite wall, gravity (and friction) makes it decrease. At a certain point no more momentum is left, and gravity pulls the boarder back down.

rises up until gravity's pull manages to overcome his or her momentum.

At the 2010 Olympics, Wescott was able to make good use of two key forces. He got just enough friction to help him control his board while not slowing him down much. At the same time, gravity's downward pull gave him the velocity he needed for victory. Of course, Wescott was able to do this because he was a very skilled boarder.

From Snow to Water

Actually, snowboarders get much of the slipperiness they need from friction! As the snowboard moves, any part of it that touches the snow meets up with friction. But friction always produces some heat. This heat melts the little bit of snow that is in contact with the board. So a snowboard gliding downhill is actually sliding on a very thin layer of water. This layer reduces the friction between the board and the snow. In other words, it works like oil between the parts of a machine.

There's another way the creation of the thin layer of water helps the snowboarder. Fresh, powdery snow offers a lot of friction. This makes it hard to go fast. The friction that produces the layer of water can also make the surface of the snow a little harder. So the board can go a little faster.

Getting Hot with Friction

Here's an easy way to see the connection between friction and heat. All you have to do is rub your hands together. After a while, they start to feel warm. This is because the friction between the two hands naturally produces heat. Rub them harder, and you will feel more heat.

Turning and Stopping

Making a quick turn with the snowboard flat on the snow can be very hard because there is a lot of friction. Skilled snowboarders often like to carve turns instead. They shift their weight and lean into the turn so that just one edge of the board touches the snow. Done correctly, this produces a quick turn. Since only the edge of the snowboard touches the snow, there is much less friction to slow down the board.

Friction also helps sideslipping work. In sideslipping, a boarder turns the board sideways and makes it dig into the snow. This increases the friction on the board, which helps to slow the board down.

From Motion to Heat

The heat produced by friction between a snowboard and the snow is actually **energy**. Energy comes in many forms. Energy can be changed from one form to another, but it cannot be created or destroyed.

When friction produces heat, it does not create the heat out of nothing. Instead, the heat has to come from changing some other form of energy. One very important form of energy for snowboarding is **kinetic energy**.

Kinetic energy is the energy of a moving object. Snowboarders gliding downhill have kinetic energy. When

Mathieu Bozzetto of France leans into a turn during a parallel giant slalom race.

they slow down, their kinetic energy drops. It doesn't simply disappear. Much of it turns into heat connected with friction.

Another important form of energy is **potential energy**. This is stored energy. Because of gravity, a snowboarder standing still at the top of a slope has potential energy. As the boarder goes downhill, the potential energy turns into kinetic energy. Friction changes some of this kinetic energy into heat energy. Then, when the boarder slows down and stops, more heat energy is produced. But not all the kinetic energy turns into heat. When the board sprays snow around, that action uses some of the kinetic energy.

Snowboarders doing tricks in half-pipes keep changing potential energy into kinetic energy and back again. They start at the top, with lots of potential energy. This turns into kinetic energy as they ride down into the pipe. As they go back up, the kinetic energy turns into potential energy. When they reach their highest point, they are not moving at all. They have no kinetic energy, but again lots of potential energy. As they start to go back down, the cycle starts again.

When a snowboarder stops, some of the boarder's kinetic energy goes to spray snow around.

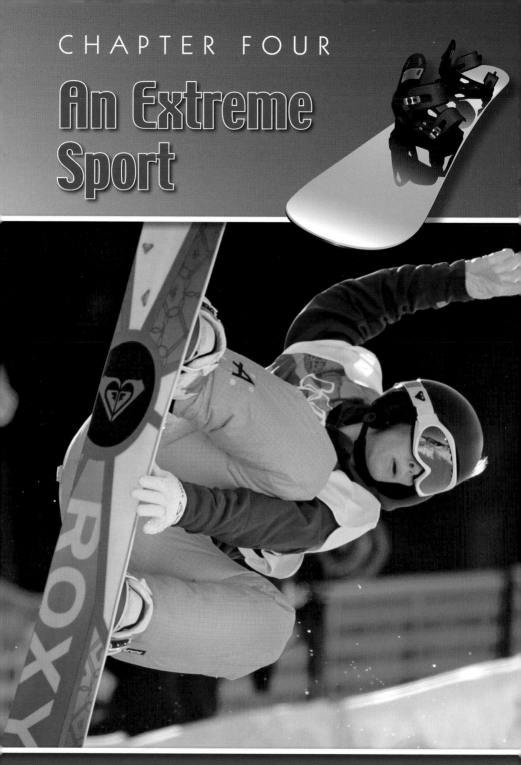

CHAPTER FOUR

An Extreme Sport

Gold-medal winner Torah Bright of Australia competes in the women's half-pipe at the 2010 Olympics.

Snowboarding is called an extreme sport. There is a reason for that. Snowboarding can be very dangerous.

Boarders moving at high speed have a lot of kinetic energy. This can be a problem when accidents happen. One boarder might run into another. Or a boarder might fall or crash into a rock, a tree, or the edge or wall of a half-pipe. Suddenly the boarder is no longer moving fast. But the kinetic energy cannot just vanish. Much of it goes to shake up the boarder's body. Sometimes the boarder suffers a serious injury. Among the more common serious injuries for boarders are broken bones and the head injury known as a concussion.

There are ways to reduce the chances of injury. Beginners should keep their speed down. They should not try to do too much until they practice and master the basics. All boarders should learn—and use—the safest ways to do moves, jumps, and tricks. For example, it's hard for straight legs to absorb shocks. So boarders should always keep their knees loose or bent. This lets the knees work like shock absorbers.

Boarders also should use good gear. This includes their board, boots, clothing, and protective gear. Good gear reduces the chances of being hurt by the powerful forces and forms of energy involved in snowboarding. That's not all it can do. It often improves a boarder's performance.

Risky Business

Even with the best gear, the possibility of an accident remains. The risk is especially great for boarders who like fast-paced racing or difficult tricks. This is true even for the most skilled boarders.

Kevin Pearce, shown here in a 2008 half-pipe competition, suffered a serious head injury in a snowboarding accident the next year.

Australia's Torah Bright took part in the women's half-pipe at the 2010 Olympics. A few weeks before, however, she had three injuries during practice. First, she hurt her jaw. Then, she got two concussions in three days. At the Olympics, she crashed on her first run in the final, and she got a score of just 5.9. (A score of 50 would be perfect.) Luckily, each boarder was allowed two runs. The better of the two was the one that counted. Bright's second run was fantastic. She got a 45 and won the gold.

Kevin Pearce was not as lucky as Bright. A star American snowboarder, he has beaten Shaun White in some events over the years. But during training at the end of 2009, Pearce hit his face on the wall of the half-pipe. He got a serious brain injury and almost died. He remained in the hospital for several months. A year after the accident, Pearce was still receiving therapy for vision and balance problems.

Be Prepared

When snowboarders do their thing, the weather is often cold, windy, or snowy. To protect themselves, they need to pick their outerwear—such as jacket, pants, and gloves—carefully. It needs to be right for the weather conditions they will meet. Also, safety gear, boots, and board should all be right for the kind of snowboarding they plan to do.

Take the boots, for example. Devices called bindings hold the boots on the board. It's important that the boots

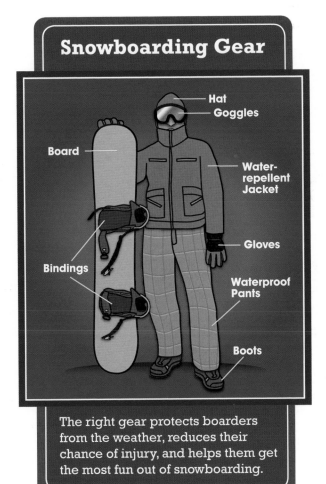

Snowboarding Gear

Hat
Goggles
Board
Water-repellent Jacket
Gloves
Bindings
Waterproof Pants
Boots

The right gear protects boarders from the weather, reduces their chance of injury, and helps them get the most fun out of snowboarding.

and bindings not be too loose, since that could reduce the rider's control of the board.

Freestyle riders do jumps and tricks in half-pipes and elsewhere. They tend to use soft boots. Soft boots weigh less and are more flexible. These features make it easier for the riders to move around in the air. People who do freeriding don't spend as much time in the air, but they also usually like the flexibility and lower weight of softer boots. Racers tend to use hard, or stiff, boots. These give better ankle protection. They also may give the boarder slightly better control of the board.

Gearing Up for Safety

Accidents happen in snowboarding. There's no way to completely avoid them. But safety gear can reduce the chances of injury.

A helmet will absorb some of the force of an impact to the head. This can't eliminate the possibility of being hurt, but it can make a really serious head injury less likely to happen. Kevin Pearce was wearing a helmet when he hit his head on a half-pipe wall in 2009. The helmet may have saved his life.

Wrist guards are another good idea. Snowboarders often fall on their hands, and this can cause a wrist injury. In fact, wrist injuries are the most common injuries in snowboarding. Wrist guards can help by absorbing some of the impact.

Shin guards and pads for knees, elbows, and hips help protect those parts of the body when a boarder falls or crashes into something. Different kinds are available. Bigger, thicker padding gives more protection. It has drawbacks—it's heavier and reduces freedom of movement. Still, boarders who love fast riding or risky tricks should consider using thick padding.

Goggles protect the eyes against wind, snow, and bright light. Boarders need to be able to see where they are going.

A safety leash straps the rider's front leg to the board. This keeps the board from accidentally getting loose and hurting someone.

If You Hit Your Head...

If you hit your head while you are snowboarding, be alert for signs of a head injury. These signs can include pain, dizziness, vision problems, or unusual behavior. Never ignore such symptoms. It's very important for anyone who has a possible head injury to be checked by a doctor and to follow the doctor's advice. If a head injury is not properly treated, the results can be very serious.

Boards Galore

Different kinds of boards are used for different types of snowboarding. A board's shape and design affect how it handles.

One important feature of a snowboard is its length. Most boards are around 55 to 65 inches (140–165 centimeters) long. Racing boards tend to be longer, stiffer, lighter, and narrower than standard boards. This helps them have less friction and cut through the snow better. Freestyle boards tend to be more flexible and a little shorter and wider than usual. These features make them better for doing tricks.

Freestyle riders tend to use a shorter board than racers.

GLOSSARY

acceleration: A change in velocity. As a measurement, it is the rate at which velocity changes.

aerodynamic: Having a shape that reduces drag on an object.

center of gravity: The point in an object where the object's weight seems to be centered.

conservation: In physics, the idea that something cannot be destroyed. For example, energy is always conserved, but it may change from one form to another.

drag: Air resistance; a force that slows an object moving through the air.

energy: In physics, the ability to do work.

force: Anything that causes a change in the velocity of an object, such as a push or a pull.

freeriding: A type of snowboarding in which boarders ride out in the countryside, over natural terrain.

freestyle: A type of snowboarding that involves doing jumps and tricks in half-pipes and elsewhere.

friction: A force resisting the movement of an object across a surface.

gravity: A force that pulls objects toward the center of Earth.

half-pipe: A long U-shaped structure on a slope used for doing freestyle aerial tricks. It looks something like the bottom half of a big pipe.

kinetic energy: The energy of a moving object.

mass: The amount of matter in an object.

momentum: A measure of an object's motion. It equals the object's mass multiplied by its velocity.

physics: The branch of science dealing with matter and energy. Scientists who work in physics are called physicists. They study such things as moving objects.

potential energy: Stored energy.

resistance: Opposition to the movement of an object.

trick: In snowboarding, a maneuver done while riding a snowboard.

velocity: In physics, the speed and direction of a moving object. Some people use the word to mean simply "speed."

FIND OUT MORE

BOOKS

Figorito, Marcus. *Friction and Gravity: Snowboarding Science*. New York: Rosen, 2009.

Fitzpatrick, Jim. *Snowboarding*. Ann Arbor, MI: Cherry Lake, 2009.

Gustaitis, Joseph Alan. *Snowboard*. New York: Crabtree, 2010.

Phelan, Glen. *Science Quest: An Invisible Force: The Quest to Define the Laws of Motion*. Washington, DC: National Geographic Children's Books, 2006.

Sandler, Michael. *Cool Snowboarders*. New York: Bearport, 2010.

WEBSITES

www.abc-of-snowboarding.com/learn-snowboarding
This site has lots of information about all aspects of snowboarding, including how to get started, safety tips, and details on styles and tricks.

www.adventuresportsonline.com/ snowboardglossary.htm
Snowboarding uses a lot of special words. This site explains many of them.

www.howstuffworks.com/outdoor- activities/snow-sports/snowboarding.htm
This webpage on the HowStuffWorks site describes the basics of snowboarding and talks about some famous snowboarders.

www.nsf.gov/news/special_reports/olympics/snowboarding.jsp
This page of the website of the National Science Foundation has a video showing how snowboarders use gravity and balance to do their half-pipe tricks.

www.ussnowboarding.com
This is the site of the U.S. Snowboarding Team. It includes information about team athletes and events in which they compete, as well as general information about the sport.

INDEX

acceleration, 13–14
air resistance (drag), 16
Anderson, Jamie, **6**

balance, 10, 13, 19
boards, **27**, 29, **29**
Bozzetto, Mathieu, **22**
Bright, Torah, **24**, 26

carving (turns), 15, **15**, 22, **22**
center of gravity, 9–11, **11**
conservation of energy, 23, **23**

Double McTwist 1260, 6, 7
drag. See air resistance (drag)

Earth (planet), 7, 8–9, 14, 17
energy, 22–23, **23**, 25

first law of motion, 8
force (physics), 7, 8–9, 13–14,
    15, 16–17, 19, 21
freeriding, 13, 28
friction, 19, **20**, 21, 22–23

gear and equipment, 25, **27**,
    27–29, **29**
Gelfland, Alan "Ollie," 7
gravity, 7, 8, 9, 10, 13, 14, 16,
    20, 21, 23

half-pipe (snowboarding), **4**, **5**, 5–6,
    7, 8, **20**, 20–21, 23, **24**, 25, 26,
    26, 28
heat, 21, 22–23
Holland, Nate, 19

injuries, 15, 25–26, **26**, **27**, 28, 29

jumps, 6, 7, **12**, 13, 19, 20, 25, 28

kinetic energy, 22–23, **23**, 25

mass, 10, 13–14, 17, 20
McGill, Mike, 7
momentum, **20**, 20–21

Newton, Isaac, 8, 13, 16
Nicoll, Mercedes, **4**

Olympic Games. See Winter Olympics

parallel giant slalom, 13, **15**, **22**
Pearce, Kevin, 26, **26**, 28
potential energy, 23
Powell, Darren, 16

rest (physics), 8
Ricker, Maëlle, **12**, 19
Robertson, Mike, 19

safety, **17**, 25, **27**, 27–28
Sauerbreij, Nicolien, **15**
second law of motion, 13–14, 15
seesaw, 10
sideslipping, 16–17, 22
snowboard cross, **12**, 13, **18**, 19
speed, 5, 8, 9, **11**, 13, 15, 16, **17**,
    19, 20, 25

third law of motion, 16–17
traversing, 15
tricks, 5, 6, 7, 13, 20, 23, 25, 28, 29
turns, 13, 14–15, **15**, 22, **22**

velocity, 9, 13, 16, 20–21

weather, 19, 27
weight, 9, 10, 13, 14, 15, 22
Wescott, Seth, **18**, 19, 21
White, Shaun, 5, **5**, 6, 7
Winter Olympics, **4**, **5**, 5–6, **12**, **18**,
    19, 21, **24**, 26
Winter X Games, **6**

About the Author

Richard Hantula has written, edited, and translated books and articles on science and technology for more than three decades. He was the senior U.S. editor for the *Macmillan Encyclopedia of Science*.

19.95